1st Recital Series

FOR Bb CLARINET

Including works of:
- James Curnow
- Craig Alan
- Douglas Court
- Mike Hannickel
- Timothy Johnson
- Ann Lindsay

Solos for Beginning
through Early Intermediate
level musicians

CURNOW® MUSIC

EXCLUSIVELY DISTRIBUTED BY
HAL•LEONARD® CORPORATION
7777 W. BLUEMOUND RD. P.O. BOX 13819 MILWAUKEE, WI 53213

T0057439

Edition Number: CMP 0685.02

1st Recital Series
Solos for Beginning through Early Intermediate level musicians
Clarinet

ISBN: 90-431-1679-3

CD Accompaniment tracks performed by Becky Shaw

CD number: 19.023-3 CMP

Foreword

High quality solo/recital literature that is appropriate for performers playing at the Beginner through Early Intermediate skill levels is finally here! Each of the **1st RECITAL SERIES** books is loaded with exciting and varied solo pieces that have been masterfully composed or arranged for your instrument.

Included with the solo book is a professionally recorded CD that demonstrates each piece. Use these examples to help develop proper performance practices. There is also a recording of the accompaniment alone that can be used for performance (and rehearsal) when a live accompanist is not available. A separate Piano Accompaniment book is available [edition nr. CMP 0751.02].

Table of Contents

☐ *Solo with accompaniment*

■ *Accompaniment*

Bb CLARINET

1. AUTUMN LEAVES
for Kristen

Douglas Court (ASCAP)

2. CRABAPPLE CROSSING

Ann Lindsay (ASCAP)

3. REFLECTIONS

Timothy Johnson (ASCAP)

4. LEGEND

Craig Alan (ASCAP)

Bb CLARINET

5. DANSE HARLEQUIN

Mike Hannickel (ASCAP)

Bb CLARINET

J. S. Bach
6. AIR from SUITE #3
"AIR on the G STRING"

Arr. **Ann Lindsay** (ASCAP)

7. RIVERSIDE PROMENADE

Bb CLARINET

Douglas Court (ASCAP)

W. A. Mozart
8. AVE VERUM CORPUS

Arr. **Timothy Johnson** (ASCAP)

Bb CLARINET

9. CHALUMEAU ON THE GO

Mike Hannickel (ASCAP)

Bb CLARINET

Georges Bizet
10. HABANERA
from
Carmen

Arr. **James Curnow** (ASCAP)

11. BARBARA ALLEN Arr. **Mike Hannickel** (ASCAP)

15

12. SOARING

James Curnow (ASCAP)